A SOUVENIR BOOK

NATIONAL MUSEUM
OF THE
AMERICAN INDIAN

REMEMBERING THE FUTURE

IN 1989, WHEN CONGRESS CREATED THE National Museum of the American Indian as part of the Smithsonian Institution, certain outcomes seemed to lie far in the future. Most mirage-like of all was the new museum we would build on the last available site on the National Mall. We met with hundreds of Native people and communities from all over the Western Hemisphere in those early days, in an attempt to gather up the best advice and wisdom available to us. And from those meetings and consultations we compiled a set of concepts and precepts that we called *The Way of the People.* This working document became, in truth, our guide to the future, our conceptual blueprint of things to come.

The Way of the People was not a rigid set of commandments, but more an anthology of philosophical suggestions and admonishments: The museum should be different from other museums. It should connect to the earth and its surroundings. Native design should define the architecture. The voices and perspectives of Native people should inform all our work. The hundreds of thousands of objects in our collection should be treated with the deepest respect and care.

The sagacious and generous people we talked with wanted, above all, for us to make the museum a Native place, one filled with a spirit of Indian hospitality. How I wish I could have reached fifteen years into the future and plucked this souvenir book from the present day to show to them, for I think its pages reveal our fidelity to their hopes for the museum. We have created, I think, a remarkable and inviting Native place, where visitors can experience the Indian world—in which the building, the landscape, the exhibitions, and even the café, are infused with the knowledge, traditions, and vision of indigenous people, both past and present.

This small jewel of a book provides readers with a comprehensive sense of the National Museum of the American Indian. It features beautiful photographs of the new Mall building, along with brief portraits of our other sites: the George Gustav Heye Center in lower Manhattan and the Cultural Resources Center in Maryland. But the core of this book is the wondrous selection of objects from our collection and images from our photography archive. This book will call to mind, as a souvenir from the National Museum of the American Indian should, the extraordinary aesthetic and cultural achievements of the Native peoples of the Americas.

W. RICHARD WEST, JR.
(Southern Cheyenne and member of the Cheyenne and Arapaho Tribes of Oklahoma)
FOUNDING DIRECTOR

THE MUSEUM ON THE NATIONAL MALL

NMAI IN WASHINGTON, D.C.

USE COLOR AND LIGHT IN A WAY THAT MAKES USE OF THE SUN. ABSTRACT A MOUNTAIN, THE PLAINS, CANYONS; THE SKY AND THE UNDERWORLD; DESERTS, WATER, THE FOUR DIRECTIONS, THE NATURAL ELEMENTS; CEREMONY, SYMBOLISM, DESIGNS.

THE SYMBOLS DO NOT HAVE TO BE LITERAL. INDIANS ARE MASTERS AT ABSTRACTION.

—*LLOYD KIVA NEW (CHEROKEE)*

BANNER POSTS IN THE MUSEUM'S SOUTHERN WALL BRING TO MIND THE VIGAS OF PUEBLO ARCHITECTURE.

The profile of the NMAI dome distinguishes it from the neoclassical domes of the Capitol and other buildings along the National Mall, recalling instead the low, stepped structures of pre-Columbian Mexico and Central America. Cast-glass sconces designed by Ramona Sakiestewa (Hopi) for the museum's main theater recall the phases of the moon and help evoke a traditional setting for Native storytelling—a clearing in the woods under a bright night sky.

DESIGNED IN CONSULTATION WITH NATIVE American groups throughout the Western Hemisphere, the National Museum of the American Indian on the National Mall reflects the importance of the natural world in Native life and beliefs, and the Native appreciation for beauty and craftsmanship. The mass and curvilinear walls of the building itself recall wind-shaped rock formations. Yet the impact of the human hand can be seen in the stonework, and in other details throughout the building. ✳ Inside, colors and design motifs are inspired by objects from the museum's collections. The interior spaces are based on circles, a shape evocative of Native storytelling and government, as well as Native architecture. A woven copper screen leads visitors to the performance area of the Potomac, the building's soaring central space. The oculus in the Potomac's domed roof pays homage to the smoke holes of many Native dwellings, and offers visitors a view of the sky. Light refracted through prisms set in the south wall traces the path of the sun during the course of the day. These and other elements—the cliff-like eastern facade sheltering the main entrance, the glass wall looking out onto the water feature and the landscape—link the inside of the museum to the outside and remind us of our relationship with the larger world.

Horizontal bands of windows set in walls of Kasota stone resemble veins of quartz in a cliff face. The massive overhang sheltering the museum's east-facing entrance is inspired by natural rock formations.

THE COLLECTION

THESE OBJECTS SPEAK ACROSS THE GENERATIONS, ACROSS CULTURAL BOUNDARIES, AND ALLOW US TO SEE WHAT THE INDIAN WAY OF THINKING IS ALL ABOUT. THAT WAY OF THINKING CAN BE SEEN IN THE USE OF THE CIRCLE AS A SYMBOL OF UNITY, IN THE USE OF ANIMAL TOTEMS TO REPRESENT THE SHARING OF POWER BETWEEN THE PEOPLE AND THE ANIMAL WORLD, AND IN A DIFFERENT ATTITUDE ABOUT THE LAND—ONE THAT SEES THE EARTH AS ALIVE AND SACRED, TO BE SHARED BY ALL.... INDIANS OF EACH GENERATION FIND WAYS TO EXPRESS THEMSELVES AS INDIANS, OFTEN TRANSFORMING NATURAL RESOURCES INTO BEAUTIFUL WORKS OF CULTURAL IDENTITY.

—*RICHARD HILL, SR. (TUSCARORA)*

INKA *QUEROS* (RITUAL DRINKING CUPS) FROM THE NMAI COLLECTION, CA. A.D. 1470 TO 1821.

KWAKWAKA'WAKW (KWAKIUTL) MECHANICAL MASK, LATE 19TH C. WOOD, CLOTH, AND CORD, HEIGHT 132 CM. 11/5235

SUN, MOON, AND STARS

FOR THOUSANDS OF YEARS, NATIVE PEOPLES HAVE LOOKED TO THE SKIES TO UNDER-stand their place in the cosmos and organize their daily lives. Seasonal ceremonies marked the equinoxes and solstices, and tribes throughout the Americas used these solar cycles as guides for the best time to hunt, fish, and plant. The sun, moon, and stars are linked to stories of the origins of the universe, of different Native groups, and of heroic figures. From carved house posts that gave the name "Moon House" to the Alaskan dwelling over which they presided, to a Blackfoot robe painted with star symbols, to a stunning turquoise mosaic shield with a solar motif found in Puebla, Mexico, objects of both ceremonial and daily life evoke the great mysteries of the universe and Native peoples' spiritual relationship with its creative powers.

The face of this dramatic mask (far left) from the Northwest Coast opens to reveal another face (left), and the fabric atop the mask opens like a fan to show the course of the sun across the sky. The mask embodies the power of transformation, even as the sun gives way to the moon and summer to winter.

Native peoples of the Northwest Coast built large structures with interior house posts supporting overhead beams. These Tlingit posts feature carvings of moons with human and possibly wolf figures. The figures in the two outer posts perhaps refer to a story about a boy who, when he went looking for water, was snatched up to the moon.

TLINGIT CARVED AND PAINTED WOOD HOUSE POSTS, CA. 1830. HEIGHTS 241.3 TO 246.4 CM. 17/8012, 17/8013, 17/8014, 17/8015

MIXTEC-AZTEC
SHIELD, 15TH C.
WOOD, TURQUOISE,
AND RESIN, DIAM.
32.5 CM. 10/8708

The Mixtec culture in southern Mexico produced finely crafted work, often by order of the Aztec state, such as this ceremonial shield, a wooden solar disk inlaid with mosaic. It represents the birthplace of Huitzilopochtli (Blue Hummingbird on the Left), the Aztec god of the sun and of war. In the center of the disk, a woman floats in the sky above the god's birthplace. His birth is associated with the sun's lowest point on the horizon, when the Aztec prepared to celebrate the sun's rising rebirth.

The design, meaning, and power of an elk hide robe came to the owner, a member of the Blackfoot, in a dream that offered the power to foretell the future and promised a long, healthy life. Spots represent stars, and other details symbolize the sun, moon, and Milky Way. Tribal stories tell of Star Boy, rejected for a scar on his face, who comes to the Sun's lodge. He saves the Sun's son, Morning Star. As a reward, his scar is removed, and he becomes the Sun's messenger to the people below. He takes with him prayers and songs, raven feathers, and a soft-tanned elk skin. He instructs the people in the ways of the Sun Dance and returns to the sky, where he can be seen with Morning Star.

BLACKFOOT MEDICINE ROBE, LATE 19TH C. GLEICHEN, ALBERTA, CANADA. ELK HIDE, BEADS, METAL, HAIR, 195 X 195 CM. 13/2384

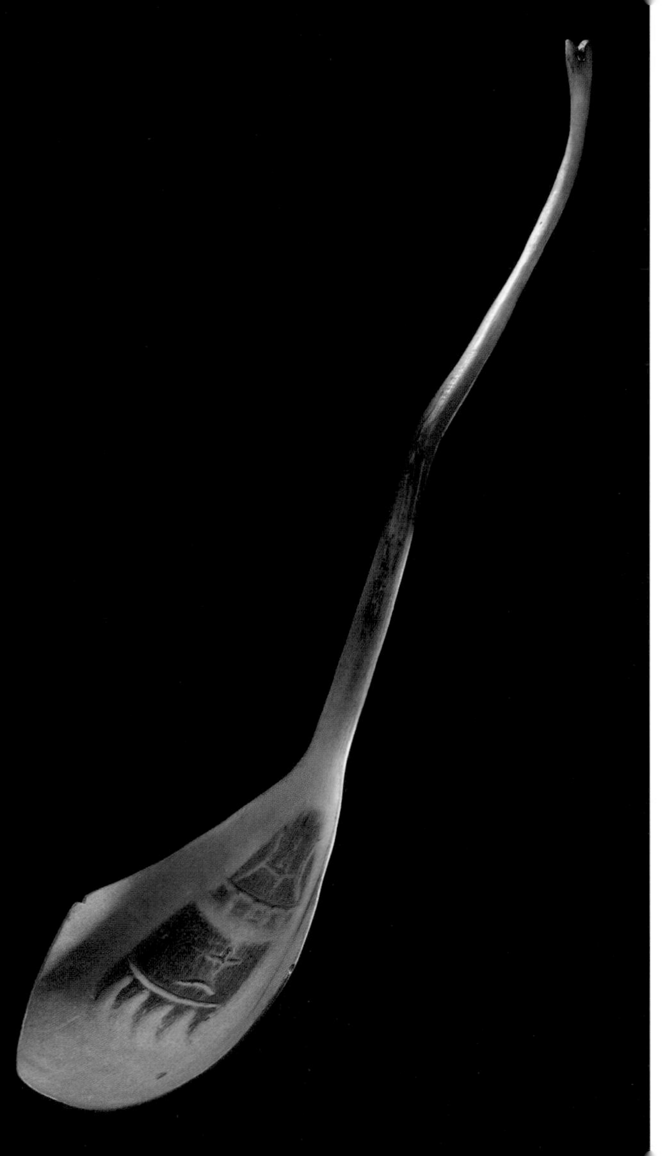

Fashioned from mountain-sheep horn and incised with a bear's claw, this spoon evokes a Native story in which seven sisters were lifted up by a huge rock known as Mato Tipi (Bear's Lodge), also called Devil's Tower, to escape a bear whose claws left the enormous fluted gashes seen on the flanks of this geologic formation. The sisters escaped into the sky and can be seen as the starry cluster known to astronomers as the Pleiades.

ARIKARA SPOON, CA. 1870. FORT BERTHOLD RESERVATION, NORTH DAKOTA. 40.7 X 7.7 CM. 13/2827

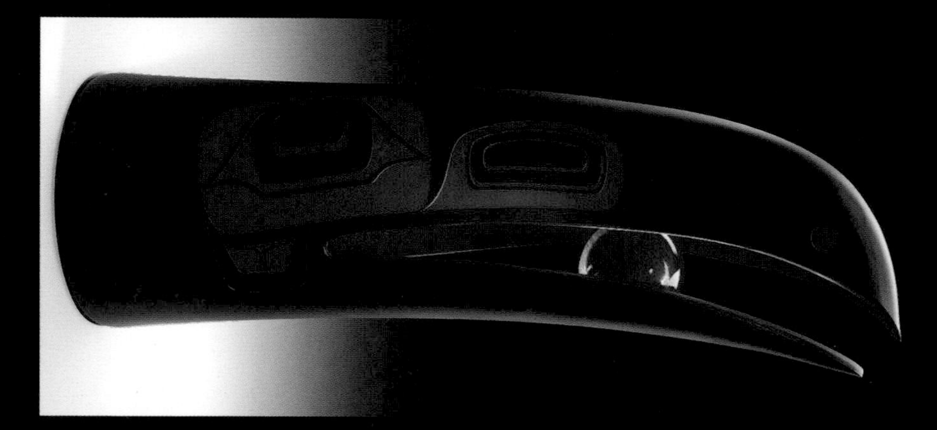

Raven, the inspiration for these sculptures by contemporary glass artists, is the great Creator, Light-bringer, and scalawag of the Northwest Coast. Long ago, families told Raven stories to their children on winter nights around the fire in the big wooden houses, including the tale of how Raven steals the sun and moon, places them in the sky, and brings light to the world. Today people live in smaller houses, or in cities, but they still share and laugh at Raven stories, and Raven still makes his appearance on artworks, on clan regalia, and on carved rattles used in dances by firelight or stage light.

PRESTON SINGLETARY (TLINGIT, B. 1963), *RAVEN STEALS THE SUN,* 2003. BLOWN AND SAND-CARVED GLASS. 26/3273

ED ARCHIE NOISE CAT (SALISH, B. 1959), *RAVEN STEALS THE MOON*, 2003. CAST-GLASS. 26/3228

ANIMAL POWERS

NATIVE PEOPLES STAND IN CLOSE RELATIONSHIP TO THE ANIMALS WHO SHARE their lands. In addition to providing humans with materials for food and items of daily life, animals possess ineffable power and play an integral role in Native spirituality. Animals from sky, sea, and land participated in the creation of the world and human life, and appear in dreams as emissaries of the spiritual realm. To many Arctic hunters, for example, the wearing of elaborate hats (such as the one pictured on p. 25) expressed a kind of sacred covenant with the natural and spiritual worlds. A hunter wearing special attire would honor the spirits of the animals who were the source of food and clothing for generations of northern peoples. In turn, animals treated with respect and dignity would offer themselves to the hunter as a willing sacrifice and renewable resource. As a visible symbol of this sacred pact, such a wooden hunting hat embodies the most profound of cultural and spiritual values.

Feline images have long been depicted in Native objects as emblematic of power, grace, speed, stealth, and deity. Two large cats of striking appearance—the jaguar and the puma—are represented in these ceramics from Central and South America.

TIWANAKU CENSER WITH PUMA SHAPE, A.D. 600–900. BOLIVIA. POTTERY, PAINT, HEIGHT 21.5 CM. 20/6314

NICOYA JAGUAR EFFIGY VESSEL, A.D. 1200–1400. COSTA RICA. POTTERY, PAINT, HEIGHT 35.6 CM. 19/4896; MOCHE STIRRUP SPOUT VESSEL OF CROUCHING JAGUAR HOLDING A MAN, 200 B.C.–A.D. 100. PERU. POTTERY, PAINT, HEIGHT 18.4 CM. 5/1888

The buffalo, or bison, provided hides for clothing and shelter (tipis) as well as food for Plains Indians, notably the Sioux (the Dakota, Lakota, and Nakota). Their ceremonies invoked the spirit and power of Pte Oyate, the ancestral Buffalo Nation whose territory lay beneath the earth before its people were tricked into emerging onto the surface. Buffalo headdresses and drums, heartbeat of the nation, were used to express thanks for the providential buffalo and to revel in the many blessings it brought—blessings that were nearly voided by the massive slaughter of herds by market gunners in the 1800s.

SIOUX BUFFALO HEADDRESS AND DRUM, 19TH C. 18/278 AND 26/2492

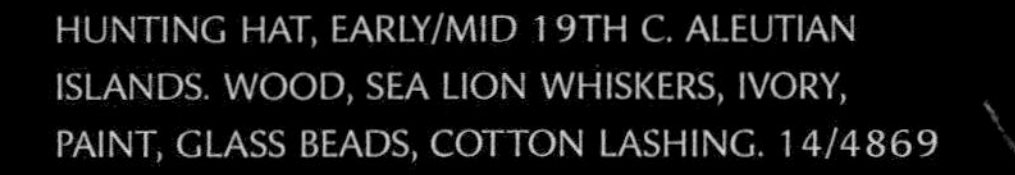

HUNTING HAT, EARLY/MID 19TH C. ALEUTIAN ISLANDS. WOOD, SEA LION WHISKERS, IVORY, PAINT, GLASS BEADS, COTTON LASHING. 14/4869

Driftwood, when scraped thin, steamed, and bent into a conical shape, was fashioned into hats for hunters of otter and other sea mammals along the Bering Sea coast of Alaska and the Aleutian Islands. The overhanging brim cut glare from reflected sunlight, and the beads, sea lion whiskers, painted designs, and carved ivory side plaques called volutes helped give the hat a larger purpose: to honor the animals and invoke spirits that would safely guide the hunters as they ventured out in kayaks and *baidarkas*.

Lone Buffalo
dance
White Horse
Cheyenne
dance
dance
Medicine
Lodges
White Cloud
Big Chief
Little Blanket
Chief

CEREMONIAL NATIONS

THROUGH CEREMONY, WITH ITS PROFOUND AND COMPLEX RITUAL PROCESS, NATIVE peoples from the Arctic to the tip of South America celebrate and renew their reciprocal relationship with a world that is seen as alive and sacred, and give thanks to the creative powers. In the ceremonial space, dancers, drummers, singers, and speakers reenact ancient stories and summon ancestral spirits. The Sun Dance, the preeminent religious ceremony of Plains tribes, has as its cynosure a circular lodge that represents the cosmos in miniature. With the sound of an eagle-bone whistle, the rhythm of the drum, and the singing of prayers, the sacred drama re-creates the world and recognizes the necessity for participants to give of themselves to maintain the great cycle of life. Despite attempts at suppression and outright banning of Native ceremonies by the U.S., Canadian, and other governments, such cultural expressions survived, and ceremonial life has been reinvigorated in recent years.

PROBABLY LITTLE CHIEF (SOUTHERN CHEYENNE, 1854–1923), *SUN DANCE ENCAMPMENT.* WATERCOLOR, INK, AND PENCIL ON PAPER, 59.5 X 65.8 CM. 11/1706

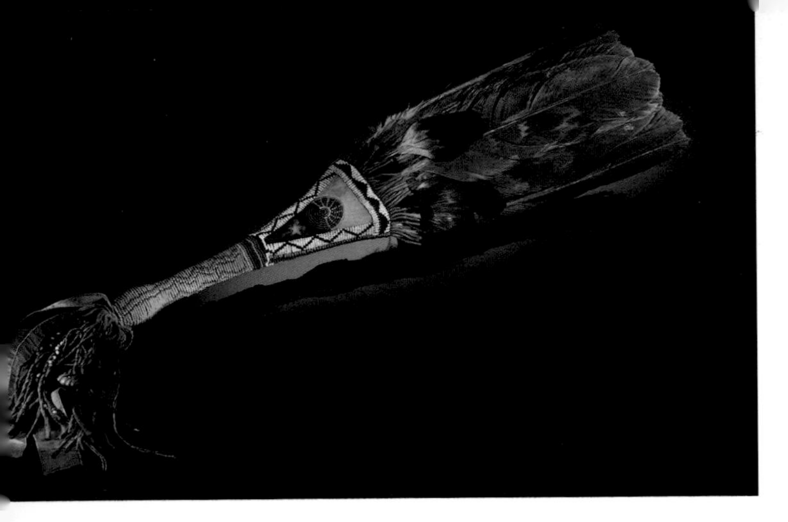

The handle of this fan holds a star, likely the Morning Star, trailing the beadwork sun as it rises against a yellow background. Tail feathers of a golden eagle evoke that bird's role as a messenger to the Creator. Fans similar to this are used in ceremonies of the Native American Church. Such fans transfer the power of cedar smoke and peyote, used sacramentally, to participants in the ceremony. Within the church, the Comanche practice a unique ceremony called the Big Moon Ceremony.

COMANCHE MEDICINE FAN, CA. 1880. FEATHER, ANIMAL HIDE, WOOD, CLOTH, BEADS, LENGTH 68.6 CM. 2/1617

A Mapuche *kultrung,* or drum, from Chile is the classical instrument of shamans called *machis,* who wear special *makuñ,* or ponchos, indicating rank. Machis sing and play the ceremonial drum, whose painted design refers to the four directions of the world, as they mediate between the natural and supernatural realms.

MAPUCHE *KULTRUNG* (DRUM) WITH STICK AND *MAKUÑ* (PONCHO), EARLY 20TH C. 17/5797 AND 17/6736

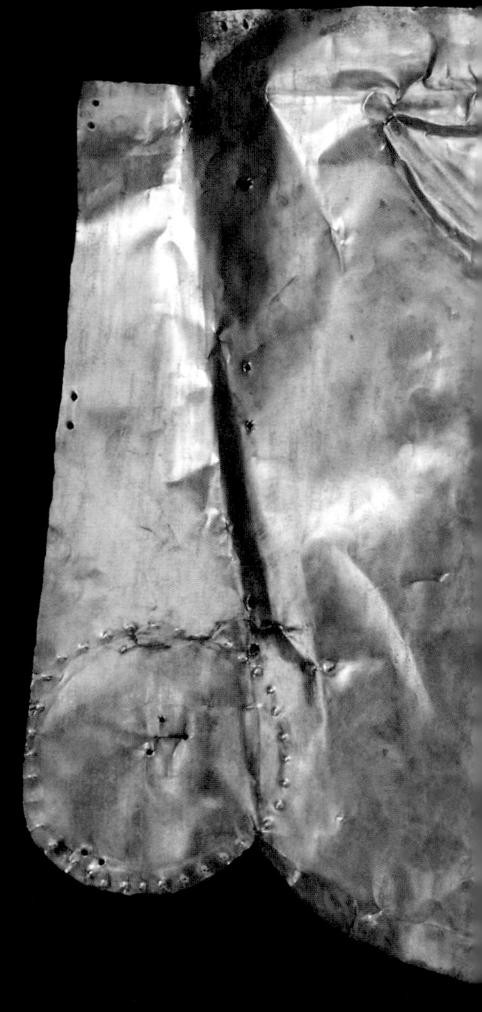

CHIMU MASK, CA. A.D.1200–1400.
PERU. GOLD, TURQUOISE. 18/4291

A collection of contemporary Maya bowls made from gourds reflects ancient patterns and uses. Painted and lacquered ones were reserved for chocolate drinks poured as an offering to Tzuultaq'a, the spirit of mountains and valleys. Even now, a woman of authority will offer a toast to visitors, and her helpers will serve the chocolate drink to them in small bowls. The bowls are carried wrapped up in the type of cloth pictured here.

MAYA PAINTED AND LACQUERED GOURD BOWLS AND COTTON CLOTH WRAPPING, CA. 1990. 25/5162

For traditional Plains Indians, smoking sacred pipes plays an important role in religious ceremonies. This tobacco cutting board is decorated with brass tacks in a manner similar to Blackfeet parfleches. The outer sides hold parallel lines, and an inner edging is formed from four main elements constructed of two triangles touching a central diamond. The "beaver tail" knife case is made of tanned deerhide and decorated in a stepped pyramid beadwork design. The double-edged steel knife blade was a popular early trade item. Indian people usually made the wooden handles.

BLACKFEET TOBACCO CUTTING BOARD. WOOD, BRASS TACKS, 30 X 30 CM. 22/1807; BLACKFEET KNIFE AND CASE. CASE LENGTH 52 CM. 11/7037

FACES OF NATIVE AMERICA

FROM AN ARRESTING CENTURY-OLD PORTRAIT OF RENOWNED LEADER Tatanka Yotanka (Sitting Bull, Hunkpapa Lakota), to a contemporary photograph of Alaskan Tatiana M. Andrew (Yup'ik), to dancers at a powwow in Washington, D.C., the images on the following pages reflect the diversity of Native America. They also illustrate the resilience with which indigenous peoples have kept their cultures alive. In 2001, for example, Ka'apor leaders won a major victory by convincing the Brazilian government to expel illegal loggers from their rain forest reserve in northeastern Brazil. Members of several villages chose to move to the southern border of their land where they built a new village to keep watch against further invasions. The photograph on pp. 38–39 shows these Ka'apor in their new settlement, hands clasped in pride and commitment. Numbering in the tens of millions, Native people live throughout the Western Hemisphere—in its most remote places and its biggest cities—and continue to enrich all our lives with their spirited presence and cultural achievements.

ALBUMEN PRINT OF BIG SPOTTED HORSE (PAWNEE), LATE 19TH CENTURY. PROBABLY OKLAHOMA.
PHOTO BY JOHN K. HILLERS. P03357

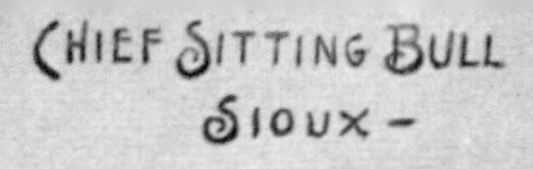
CHIEF SITTING BULL
SIOUX -

TATIANA M. ANDREW (YUP'IK), 2004.

COLORED PRINT OF TATANKA YOTANKA (SITTING BULL, HUNKPAPA LAKOTA), 1898. OMAHA, NEBRASKA. PHOTO BY FRANK A. RINEHART OR ADOLPH F. MUHR. PO4405

MEMBERS OF THE KA'APOR COMMUNITY OF XIEPIHUNRENDÁ, RESERVA INDÍGENA ALTO TURIAÇU, MARANHÃO, BRAZIL, JULY 2003.

ROXANNE SWENTZELL (SANTA CLARA PUEBLO) CREATED A BAS-RELIEF TO GRACE THE CANYON-LIKE CORRIDOR WEST OF THE POTOMAC, THE MALL MUSEUM'S DOMED CENTRAL SPACE. THE ARTIST FIRST SCULPTED THE SIX LARGER-THAN-LIFE FIGURES OF HER COMPOSITION IN CLAY, THEN CAST THEM IN BRONZE.

TLINGIT ARTIST NATHAN JACKSON AT WORK ON THE 20-FOOT-TALL CEDAR TOTEM POLE THAT IS ONE OF THE LANDMARK WORKS IN THE MALL MUSEUM.

CONTESTANTS IN MEN'S TRADITIONAL DANCE AT THE NMAI POWWOW ON THE NATIONAL MALL, WASHINGTON, D.C., 2002.

THE NATIVE AESTHETIC

A RICH TRADITION OF CREATIVITY MANIFESTS BOTH TRIBAL AND PERSONAL identity in the objects that Indian people fashion. Diverse Native cultures have produced varied treasures, including intricate and massive carvings from the Northwest Coast of North America; elegantly painted and beaded hides and garments from the North American Plains; pottery and basketry from the southwestern United States; textiles and gold from the Andean cultures; elaborate featherwork from Amazonia; and paintings by contemporary Native American artists. With a powerful sense of design and form, Native art is a dynamic force that allows individual and community vision to evolve and thrive. Indian artists became renowned for their beadwork, for example, after European trade introduced glass beads. Designs once fashioned with quills or paint now embodied community identity and personal innovations in shimmering beaded patterns. Carriers of knowledge and expressions of beauty, the objects created by the ancestors helped keep Native cultures alive and continue to strengthen and inspire indigenous peoples today.

ANISHINAABE (OJIBWE OR CHIPPEWA) QUILLED BIRCHBARK OBJECTS FROM THE NMAI COLLECTION.

Beaded bags are in the line of a long tradition of Plateau tribes' craft. Earlier woven bags of hemp and cornhusk to carry and store root crops were modified to hold personal items. Then European influences arrived by way of glass beads, wool trade cloth, and cotton. A bag from a Yakama maker (left) sets animals and flowers in a sinuous background pattern. A Umatilla bag of a slightly later date (below) portrays a warrior, his horse, and a bird in a beaded appliqué style.

KLIKITAT, YAKAMA NATION, BEADED BAG, CA. 1900. GLASS BEADS, COTTON, WOOL TRADE CLOTH, LEATHER, 42.5 X 36.2 CM. 13/8466; UMATILLA BEADED BAG, EARLY 20TH C. GLASS BEADS, DEERSKIN, WOOL TRADE CLOTH, LINEN, COTTON THREAD, 25.4 X 23.3 CM. 21/7902

For centuries and longer, baskets were essential to Native life. Food was stored and cooked in them. Many things were carried in them—from babies to firewood. Apache olla baskets were coiled so tightly that they could be used to carry water day after day. Materials, designs, and shapes varied from community to community, and the basket of an Apache living in a desert might little resemble a Penobscot pack basket used in the forests of Maine. Native baskets are now eagerly collected, and students are keen to learn the art and craft. They might keep in mind the insight of a California Native teacher, "A basket is a song made visible."

Both practical and beautiful, cradleboards (right) made to carry and protect infants symbolize the love and nurture of children, and the continuance of family and cultural traditions.

WHITE MOUNTAIN APACHE BASKET, CA. 1900. ARIZONA. HEIGHT 58 CM. 21/5350
CRADLEBOARDS FROM THE NMAI COLLECTION.

CONTEMPORARY VISIONS

THIS SECTION HIGHLIGHTS THE CONTINUING BEAUTY AND POWER OF NATIVE artistic expression, and the resurgence of indigenous culture. The compelling works in the following pages—humorous, ironic, serene, spiritual—offer varied views of the diverse realities of contemporary Native American experience, reflecting their creators' beliefs, identities, visions, and responses to the challenges of enormous social and political change. Indians have long used a wry, ironic sensibility, with connections to the timeless trickster figures of Native oral narrative, as a survival tool. Shared across geographical divides and tribal boundaries, this sensibility comes into play as Native peoples confront obstacles or explore issues of identity. Many contemporary Indian artists reinterpret old symbols or anneal them into abstract expressions. Each generation renews—in both artworks and the objects of daily life—a rich tradition of creativity.

After World War II, potters from Acoma Pueblo accelerated a revival that had begun in the 1870s of a still older black-and-white style that itself dated to the A.D. 850–1275 period. The new movement spread to hundreds of potters who accepted the old style but added innovations in form and line.

ACOMA POTTERY (FROM TOP): LUCY LEWIS, 1962, HEIGHT 20.6 CM. 25/5415; MARIE Z. CHINO, 1963, HEIGHT 18.3 CM. 25/8853; DOROTHY TORIVIO, 1986, HEIGHT 9.3 CM. 25/5816; RACHEL CONCHO, 1987, HEIGHT 7 CM. 25/5817. ALL, INDIAN ARTS AND CRAFTS BOARD COLLECTION, DEPARTMENT OF THE INTERIOR, AT THE NATIONAL MUSEUM OF THE AMERICAN INDIAN, SMITHSONIAN INSTITUTION.

For more than six generations, ironworkers from the Iroquois Confederacy nations have assembled frameworks for skyscrapers and bridges. This tough and dangerous work also inspires humor, as in an artist's highly decorated hardhat. An ironworker before becoming a painter, Richard Glazer-Danay was born in Coney Island, New York, and raised in Hollywood, California. The influences of those places come through in his art by the use of bright colors, references to pop culture, and satire. *Pink Buffalo Hat* is painted with personal images and symbols of a candied apple (alluding to New York), turtles (his clan), Betty Boop, and a pink buffalo (an Indian version of the pink elephant).

With works such as *The American Indian* (right), Fritz Scholder moved the representation of Indian people beyond clichés and preconceived ideas, earning a worldwide reputation and status as a major influence on contemporary American Indian art.

RICHARD GLAZER-DANAY (MOHAWK, TURTLE CLAN, B. 1942), *PINK BUFFALO HAT,* CA. 1983. OIL PAINT ON PLASTIC CONSTRUCTION HAT. INDIAN ARTS AND CRAFTS BOARD COLLECTION, DEPARTMENT OF THE INTERIOR, AT THE NATIONAL MUSEUM OF THE AMERICAN INDIAN, SMITHSONIAN INSTITUTION. 25/7093

FRITZ SCHOLDER (LUISEÑO, B. 1937), *THE AMERICAN INDIAN,* 1970. OIL ON CANVAS, 153 X 107.4 CM. INDIAN ARTS AND CRAFTS BOARD COLLECTION, DEPARTMENT OF THE INTERIOR, AT THE NATIONAL MUSEUM OF THE AMERICAN INDIAN, SMITHSONIAN INSTITUTION. 26/1056

Carlos Jacanamijoy grew up in a Quechua-speaking Inga community amid the color and light of the rain forest of the eastern slope of the Colombian Andes. He says of his technique, as in this painting: "I am able to find new paths and create, for example, the language of symbols and geometry in the collective art of my people. My pictures flow from the experiences of everyday life."

CARLOS JACANAMIJOY (INGA, B. 1964), *ROSE IN TRIBUTE,* 2001. OIL ON CANVAS, 170 X 140 CM. 26/1565

JOE FEDDERSEN (COLVILLE, B. 1953), *TIRE,* 2003. SANDBLASTED BLOWN GLASS, HEIGHT 36.8 CM. 26/2874

Take a traditional shape, but work it in a new medium. Pay homage to an old design, but turn a modern one on its head. In works such as the sandblasted blown glass *Tire*, Joe Feddersen explores the basketry designs of his people in a fresh approach—energized by his interest in investigating signs—that places a contemporary grid over the older pattern. Others of his similar pieces are *Chain Link*, *Parking Lot*, *High Voltage Tower*, and *Freeway with HOV.*

Allan Houser is often called the father of contemporary Native American sculpture, and his powerful yet tender *Reverie* makes mother and child one united sculptural form and emotional being.

ALLAN HOUSER (WARM SPRINGS CHIRICAHUA APACHE, 1914–1994), *REVERIE,* 1981. BRONZE, 63.5 X 58.4 X 33 CM. 25/7238

THE GEORGE GUSTAV HEYE CENTER

NMAI IN NEW YORK

FEW PEOPLE CAN SAY: I KNOW EXACTLY WHERE I CAME FROM.

BUT WE WERE ALWAYS HERE.

—*DORIS LEADER CHARGE* (*ROSEBUD SIOUX*)

THE CULTURAL RESOURCES CENTER

NMAI IN MARYLAND

GOING INTO THE CULTURAL RESOURCES CENTER IS LIKE GOING INTO A CHURCH,

BECAUSE THERE ARE SACRED OBJECTS HERE.

—*CLAYTON OLD ELK* (*CROW*)

DERRICK DAVIS (HOPI/CHOCTAW) PERFORMING A HOOP DANCE AT THE OPENING OF THE HEYE CENTER.

THE GEORGE GUSTAV HEYE CENTER, HOUSED IN THE ALEXANDER HAMILTON U.S. Custom House, stands at the southern tip of Manhattan, an area rich in history. New York's famous Broadway, which begins in front of the Heye Center, follows the Wiechquaekeck Trail, an old Algonquian trade route leading north along the Hudson River. In 1624, Dutch merchants negotiated with Canarsie Indian leaders in nearby Battery Park. And in 1790, in a failed bid to win George Washington's support for the city as the site of the new nation's capital, New York commissioned construction of a grand, red brick home for the U.S. president on the site now occupied by the Custom House. ✷ The Custom House, designed by architect Cass Gilbert (1859–1934) and opened in 1907, is a landmark in its own right—one of New York's most lavish Beaux Arts buildings. Every detail of its architecture speaks to the image of America as a nation taking its destined place in the world. Named in honor of the wealthy New Yorker whose extraordinary collections are the cornerstone of the National Museum of the American Indian, the Heye Center presents original and traveling exhibitions and an extensive calendar of public programs, including a world-renowned Native American Film and Video Festival. ✷ Across New York Harbor, the Statue of Liberty and the Ellis Island Immigration Museum tell the stories of the people who came to the Americas. The Heye Center tells the stories of the people who have always been here.

Once a monument to national wealth and power, the Alexander Hamilton U.S. Custom House in New York now serves as a stage for celebrating the strength and continuity of America's Native cultures. Figures representing America, Asia, Europe, and Africa sculpted by Daniel Chester French (1850–1931) flank the entrance to the Heye Center. Beneath the dome of the Rotunda, frescos by Reginald Marsh portray explorers of the Americas and trace the path of a ship entering New York Harbor.

THE CULTURAL RESOURCES CENTER IN SUITLAND, Maryland—conceived of as "the heart and soul" of the National Museum of the American Indian—houses the museum's collections, research, and community services programs. ✻ Spanning more than 10,000 years of history, and representing tribes and nations from throughout the Americas, from the Arctic Circle to Tierra del Fuego, the museum's holdings comprise the most comprehensive assemblage of Native cultural material in the world. The CRC offers Native spiritual and community leaders, as well as Native and non-Native scholars, access to this incomparable resource. In keeping with the belief held by many Native peoples that everything in the world has life and spiritual importance, the CRC also accommodates culturally appropriate care for the collections, alongside state-of-the-art conservation. ✻ Native consultants to the design team of the CRC asked the museum to build a home for the collections, rather than simply a storage facility. Respect for the objects and for the people who made them is reflected in such details as the nautilus-shell geometry of the roof, evocative of the natural world; the building's careful orientation to east, west, north, and south; the recurrence of design elements in sets of four, a sacred number in many Native cultures; and the ceremonial spaces in the center's Rotunda and on its wooded grounds.

The design of the CRC grew out of collaborations among NMAI staff, Native peoples from throughout the Western Hemisphere and Hawai'i, and architects, including a consortium of Native design professionals and cultural consultants. Native grasses and indigenous shrubs and trees create an unstructured landscape. The roof suggests natural spiral forms—nautilus shells, spider webs, and pine cones. Four glass blocks set in the mahogany floor of the Rotunda mark the cardinal directions and form a symbolic opening to the earth—an homage to tribes who believe they emerged from the earth.

NATIONAL GEOGRAPHIC

Smithsonian
National Museum of the American Indian

PUBLISHED BY THE NATIONAL GEOGRAPHIC SOCIETY

John M. Fahey, Jr.,
President and Chief Executive Officer
Gilbert M. Grosvenor,
Chairman of the Board
Nina D. Hoffman,
Executive Vice President

PREPARED BY THE BOOK DIVISION

Kevin Mulroy, Vice President and Editor-in-Chief
Charles Kogod, Illustrations Director
Marianne R. Koszorus, Design Director

STAFF FOR THIS BOOK

Rebecca Lescaze, Project Editor
Peggy Archambault, Art Director
R. Gary Colbert, Production Director
Richard S. Wain, Production Project Manager
Theodore B. Tucker, IV, Design Assistant

MANUFACTURING AND QUALITY CONTROL

Christopher A. Liedel, Chief Financial Officer
Phillip L. Schlosser, Managing Director
John T. Dunn, Technical Director
Vincent P. Ryan, Manager
Clifton M. Brown, Manager

CREDITS AND ACKNOWLEDGMENTS

cover (detail): Tony Abeyta, (Navajo, b. 1965), *Anthem,* 2004. Mixed media on wood panels, 26/4501

pp. 1, 2–3, back cover: Views of NMAI's museum on the National Mall.

PHOTO CREDITS

Historical images from the NMAI Photo Archives are identified where they appear by photograph or negative numbers. Sources for the remaining photographs are given here.

pp. 1, 2–3, 6, 8, 9, 10, 11, back cover, Maxwell MacKenzie. © 2004 Maxwell MacKenzie
pp. 12, 14, 16, 17, 18, 19, 20, 21, 23, 24, 29, 32, 33, 44, 47, 48, 49, 51, 52, 57, Ernest Amoroso
pp. 25, 62, 63 Katherine Fogden (Mohawk)
pp. 26, 28, 30–31, 53, 55, Walter Larrimore
pp. 37, 40, 41 Cynthia Frankenburg
pp. 38–39, João Paulo Santos Barbosa
pp. 42–43, 46, R. A. Whiteside
p. 56, photo by Richard Nicol, courtesy of Joe Feddersen
pp. 58, 61, Roy Gumpel
p. 60, David Heald

Special thanks to Suzanne G. Fox, Heidi H. McKinnon, Gerald McMaster (Plains Cree), Lou Stancari, Holly Stewart, Leslie Wheelock

Published in conjunction with the opening of the museum on the National Mall of the Smithsonian's National Museum of the American Indian, Washington, D.C., September 21, 2004.

Head of Publications, NMAI:
Terence Winch

Project Editor, NMAI:
Elizabeth Kennedy Gische

The Smithsonian's National Museum of the American Indian is dedicated to working in collaboration with the indigenous peoples of the Americas to protect and foster Native cultures throughout the Western Hemisphere. The museum's publishing program seeks to augment awareness of Native American beliefs and lifeways, and to educate the public about the history and significance of Native cultures.

For information about the Smithsonian's National Museum of the American Indian, visit the NMAI Website at www.AmericanIndian.si.edu.